# THINGS I LOVE ABOUT YOU

© Thomas Media

Founded in 2017, Thomas Media is a publisher of gift books, creative books, innovative journals, cards, notepads and stationery. Thomas Media publishes over 50 books and ancillary products per year.

© Thomas Media

**Visit us at Thomasmedia.ie**

Copyright © 2017
by Thomas Media Ltd.
Athlone, Westmeath, Ireland
All Rights Reserved
ISBN: 978-1-9998747-9-7
Printed: United States

"Things I Love About You" © Thomas Media Limited 2017. All rights reserved. No part of this kit shall be reproduced, stored in a retrieval system, or transmitted by any means – electronic, mechanical, photocopying, recording, or otherwise – without written permission from the publisher.

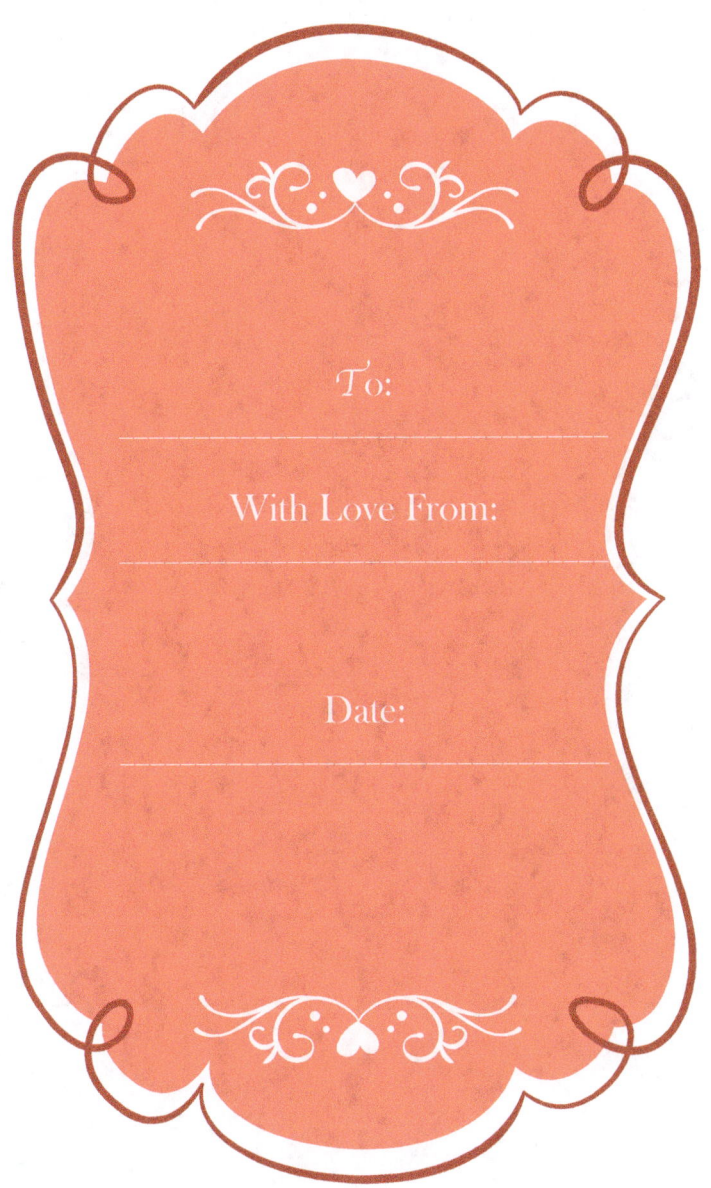

# A time that you planned a picnic.

# The little things that you do.

A time you hellped me in my career.

An awkward moment we shared together.

The time that you stopped to help someone in need.

The time that you helped someone.

A time we went for a drive in the country.




A time you wrote me a love note.

Desserts I share with you but don't want to.

Something I have been afraid to tell you.

A time you gave me a pep talk.

A time that you wrote me a song.

A time that you reminded me that you are here.

A time you wore clothes I thought were funny.

Reasons I'm proud of you.

A time that you cried.

Thoughtful things you do without being asked.

The most fun I've ever had with you.

A time we went to a concert together.

A time that you helped me finish a project.

Something I want you to know I forgave long ago.

A time that you reminded me of why I am mportant.

A time that you didn't want to say goodbye.

A time that you told me how nice I smell.

Some house jobs I wish you would do with me.

Nicknames we have for each other that I love.

Things you are passionate about in life that I love.

The times that you promised to take care of me.

Something new I'm starting to love about you is.

A time that you told me how nice I taste.

A time you ate at the restaurant you least enjoy.

Some of the sweet things you do for me are.

A time that you wrote me a poem.

The time that you held my hand when I was scared...

The time that you cleaned the garage.

One thing I've always admired about you is.

The time that you mourned with me.

A time that you changed clothing because I asked.

The times I'm most attracted to you are...

A time that you walked away, but didn't want to take your eyes off of me.

When I think of you I feel.

How I wish to strengthen in our relationship is.

A time you planned the perfect candlelight dinner for us.

A time we danced together.

A relaxing holiday I would like to share with you.

The time we had food together on the beach.

# A time you told me to stop having a pity party.

# The times that you say "Don't forget to"...

A time we took a bike ride together.

A time you got your hair cut the way I like most.

Some daily rituals I love to share with you.

A time you made me my favorite food.

## Something you did not know about me.

## A time you helped me without anyone knowing it.

A time you made me feel stronger.

A time you confided in me.

A time you scared me.

A time that you helped me brainstorm ideas.

A time that you didn't laugh at me for backing out something because of my fears.


A new activity I would like to share with you.

A time that you let me pick the game we were playing.

A time you helped me reach my goals.

A time I thought I had lost you.

A time you made me feel the happiest in the world.

A time you searched to find something I had lost.

A time I was amazed by you.

Something I'm happy we shared together.

A time your helped me when my car broke down.

Chores you do for me which I really appreciate.

A time that you admitted to being wrong.

A time we were lost together.

My idea of our future home together.

# I love you in the morning when.

# A time you dried my tears.

A time you made me face my fears.

A time others were looking but I did not care.

# A time you made me be a detective.

# A time you drew me a picture.

A time that you drove me to the doctor.

A time you tickled me.

# A time you showed me something.

# The way you are kind with me.

A time you surprised me with my favorite...

An event I would like to share with you.

A time you were the designated driver.

A time you made me ask questions.

# A time you embraced me.

# A time that you took me to a show.

A time that you let me borrow your car.

A time that you went apartment hunting with me.

# A dream I want to fulfill with you.

# A time that you complimented me to my parents.

A time that you visited me at work.

The photographs I love the most with you are.

A time that you agreed to watch that show you hate.

Something I was slow to forgive you about.

A dream I would like to share with you.

The time we first met.

A time we took a boat trip together.

A time that you surprised me with concert tickets.

The time that you proofread something for me.

The time that you something in my car for me.

Things I will work on to improve our relationship.

Some words or phrases I associate with you are.

The time that you ran to the store because I wanted.

A time that you stayed awake because I couldn't sleep.

My favorite walk together.

A funny thing we do as a couple.

A time we had fun in the sea.

A time that you planned a vacation for us.

# A time we planted something together.

# Some of the greatest strengths you have.

A time that you played board games with me.

I love that you do not mind.

A time you surprised me.

A time that you visited my parents with me.

A time you hid small presents around the house.

A game I would like to play with you.

A time that you shared something with me.

The time that you bought me my favorite magazine.

# A time you supported me.

# The time that we first kissed.

A time you kept a secret.

The time that you vowed to love me forever.

The time that you planned a surprise party for me.

A time you gave me my favorite...

The time that you made a promise and kept it.

A time you left me a small gift.

Some of the greatest weakness you have overcame.

Our favorite city breaks together.




How you have changed me for the better.




The time that you gave me a back massage.

A time that you helped me when I was hurt.

An adventure I would like to share with you.

A time I lied to you and knew you could see through it, but you said nothing.

A time you left a lovely message for me.

# Somethings we have laughed about together.

# A time that you showed me I can do it.

A time you made me remember.

A time you went looking for something I lost.

# A time you wore some of my clothing.

# The time that you prayed with me.

The time that you helped me decorate for the party.

A time that you ran to me.

A thought I would like to share with you.

A time we had fun in a swimming pool.

Times you waited for the right time.

Something I would like to help you with.

## The time that you got embarrassed in front of me.

## A time that you missed something to help me.

Sometimes I was lucky to have had you by my side.

Funny things you do that I love.

Some lyrics from our favorite song.

The first time I said "I love you".

A time that you protected me.

A time that you made me feel like royalty.

A fragrance you wear that I love.

The time that you helped me clean up after the party.

A time we visited an amusement park together.

The time you helped me pick out the perfect outfit.

How you keep me going through a tough time.










How our life would change if we won the lotto?

A time that you took me to an amusement park.

A time that we shared in the park.

## Something about you I would like to know more about.

## A time that you found the perfect clothing for me.

A time that you listened to me give you some constructive criticism.

A famous person you remind me of is.

A time that you planned a secret date.

Somethings you love and accept about me.

# A time you held me.

# The time you fed me chocolate covered strawberries.

# A time that we stopped by the side of the road.

# Some looks you give me that make me smile.

A quote that reminds me of you.

Movies I enjoy watching with you are...

A time that you helped my family and did not complain.

A time you helped me succeed.

The reason I was first attracted to you was...

A time you remembered a seemingly insignificant date.

The times that you ask "are you okay?"

A time you kissed me I'll never forget.

A time that you could have yelled at me, but didn't.

The first time you said "I love you".

The time that you cried with me.

A time we visited a new place.

My favorite summer time memory of you is...

### A poem I would like to share with you.

### The time you wiped something from my face.

### A time you drove me...

A time you made me forget.

Because of you, I...

A time that you presented me with a certificate.

A time that you left work early because I needed you.

A time you whispered to me.

A time you made me forget my fears.

# A time we went camping together.

# A future date night I would like to take you on.

I love it when you listen to my needs because...

The time that you planned the perfect Valentine's.

A time you made me laugh.

The time that you made inside jokes with me.

I love your spirit because...

I love it when you put your arms around me because...

A time you made me healthier.

A time that you complimented me to your friends.

A time we went on a romantic dinner.

A time that you let me win a game.

# A time that you asked for my opinion.

# The most excited I've ever been.

# A time you gave me good advice.

# The time you made me breakfast in bed.

I love the way you.

The most disappointed I've ever been.

A time that you watched a movie just for me.

A time that you serenaded me.

A time that you sent me funny pictures of yourself.

The happiest I've ever been.

The time that you massaged my temples to alleviate my headache.

A time that you helped me overcome my injuries.

The time that you gave me a foot massage.

The times that you love me, even when you don't like me.

A time you gave me my favorite writing instrument.

A time you told me that you wished you could take my pain.

A time that you made me feel like more than I am.

The time that you watched the sun set with me.

A time that we played in the park.

I love the way you always.

A time you let me be your teacher.

A time that you raced with me.

A time that you built a fire.

A time that you emailed me at work.

Some sentences I would like you to complete.

A list of why of reasons why I love you.

## Somethings I wish you would do more of.

## A place I would like to take you.

A time we took a plane ride together.

The time that you shocked me by coming home early.

A time we laughed together.

The time that you put yourself out for my family.

The time that you decorated the house with my favorite Christmas decor.

The song I associate with you the most is...




Some peeves I have with you.




A time you went we did something dangerous together.

A time that you helped me move.




The time that you covered my eyes when I was afraid to look.

Times you did romantic things I liked.

A time you helped me get undressed.

When I think of us I feel...

The most important thing in our relationship is...

A time you helped me toss caution to the wind.

A time that you drove me around.

A time that you made me feel like the most beautiful person in the world.



A time I lied to you and regretted it.

The part of your body I love the most is...

Secret words, phrases and things we do or say when we are alone together.

How you have made me grow as a person.

A time that you let me use your favorite...

Our perfect day together is...

A time you ran an errand for me.

An experience I would like to share with you.

A time that you stood embracing me.

A time you opened my eyes.

A memory I wish we could relive together.

The time we shared a Christmas adventure.

Little things I do to show you how much I love you.

A time that you let me plan the party.

# The time we played games on the beach.

A time that you told me I was amazing.

The time that you helped me with a cause.

The time that could have called me a "chicken", but you didn't.

A time that you gave me jewelry.

A time that you whispered sweet nothings in my ear.

A time you bought me a greeting card.

A time that you complimented me to your parents.

A time to stood by me.

I loved you the moment you...

I love it when...

A time that you missed something to sit with me.

Things I am grateful for in our relationship.

A photo I cherish.

A present I would like to get you in time.

Before I met you my life was...




A time you took me to our "first" restaurant.

A time that you told your friends/family you were too busy.

A time that you asked for my advice.

The time that you tested me before the big interview.

The qualities I see in you that I admire most are...

Why we are soul-mates...

The times that you say "be careful".

The time that you held my hand as we drove.

Something I would like to learn with you.

A moment with you I would like to relive over and over.

The thing I have always admired most is...

A restaurant I would like to take you to.

The times that you say "I love you" help me...

A time that you danced in the rain with me.

A time that you pushed me to finish something.

A time that you could have complained, but didn't.

Our favorite time of year is...

The time that you ironed my shirt.

A time that you helped me study for a test.

The funny way you...

A time you took me back to where we first kissed.

The time you kept my secrets.

The most surprised I've ever been was...

Some things I think we should introduce into our relationship.

Sometimes I wish you had been by my side.

## The time that you admitted you loved me and only me.

## A time that you dedicated a song to me.

A time that you let me have the last piece of cake.

A time that you grilled my favorite food.

The first time I saw you, I...

A time that you finished my sentences.

A song you sing to me.

Little jobs I like doing with you.

I love you in the evening when...

A challenge I would like us to take together.

A time that you planned a weekend getaway.

A favorite birthday with I celebrated with you.

A time you said something very special to me.

My most memorable moment with you has been...

The time you invited my parents over for dinner.

A time that you complimented me to my co-workers.

Some traits I have picked up from you.

A time you excited me.

A dance you thought me.

Times together I remember, that still make me smile.

Something I'm glad you know about me.

My favorite winter time memory of you is...

A time that you missed work because I needed you.

The time that you drove to the pharmacy to get my medication when I was not feeling well.

A time that you gave me money.

A time you were strict on me for my own good.

The time I'm most looking forward to are...

A time that you fixed the computer glitch.

The time that you helped me create something.

A dream I have about you.

A time that you gave me your water bottle.

The times you were strong when I was weak.

The time that you were frightened with me.

A time that you made me a surprise CD.

I love it when you kiss me because...

A time that you planned a picnic in our front yard.

The time you made something for me from scratch.

An outfit I would like to wear for you.

A time you gave me an unexpected present.

A time you took care of me.

A time that you turned up the radio when our song came on.


A time that you helped me in the middle of the night.

A time we held hands in the cold.

A time that you inspired me.

A time you selflessly helped a person.

A time you did something for me because I was tired.

# A time that you forgave me.

# The time that you laughed with me.

# Sign Up to ThomasMedia.ie

**Thomas Media is an independent publisher based in Dublin, Ireland. At Thomas Media, we are passionate about books and our readers. We would like to invite you to become a member of community and enjoy exclusive benefits. With already 25,000 happy customers worldwide, we promise you'll be in good company.**

- **Up to 50% off your next website purchases**

- **Access to free offers**

- **Birthday gifts**

- **Free shipping offers**

- **First dibs on sales**

- **& more……**

To subscribe, simply visit our website at:

http://www.thomasmedia.ie/subscribe.html

# 365 Creative Series

# ALMOST